GOLF
Tours and Detours

GOLF
Tours and Detours
Golf's greatest moments

Lawrence Levy and Brian Morgan
Foreword by Greg Norman
Last Word by Peter Cook

Salem House Publishers
Topsfield, Massachusetts

Published by Salem House Publishers, 1988,
462 Boston Street, Topsfield, Massachusetts, 01983

© Sackville Design Group Ltd, London

ISBN 0−88162−362−8

Printed and bound in Spain by Graficromo. S.A.. Cordoba

Contents

To our parents,
Joe and Ninot Levy
and Samuel and Ethel Morgan

Acknowledgements: We should like to thank Danielle Fluer
and Dorothy Morgan for their work on this book
and for helping to make it all possible

The publishers and photographers wish to express special thanks to Nikon for
their support and kind assistance in the production of this book. The excellent
photographs testify to the superior quality of Nikon's photographic equipment.

Foreword

Lawrence Levy and Brian Morgan have a great love of golf, which I think shows in their work. Like all great action photographers, they have that sixth sense which somehow gets them to the right place at the right time.

They have another quality more important from the professional golfer's point of view: they go about their business with a keen appreciation of the player's needs. I enjoy seeing good photographs, but not at the peril of disrupting my concentration.

Perhaps it is because they are keen golfers themselves that they can gauge so well the distinction between reportage and unwelcome intrusion.

They have the unusual distinction of being popular with their subjects and, as you will see in *Tours and Detours*, they are truly excellent photographers.

Greg Norman

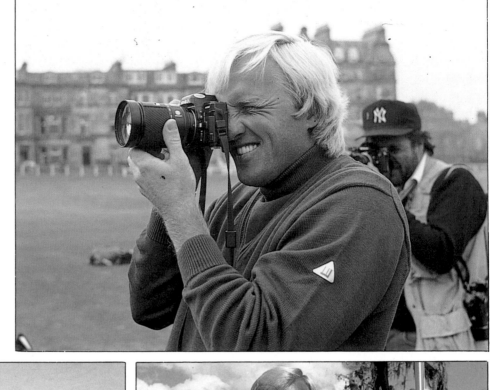

The men behind the cameras

To photographers as experienced as Brian Morgan and Lawrence Levy, the technical side of the job is second nature. The real art of action photography is more elusive – the happy knack of having the finger on the button at just the right moment. Call it foresight, inspired hunch or sheer luck, it will always be the most vital ingredient. Take these examples.

Brian was prevented by prior commitments from attending the first three rounds of the 1980 US Open at Baltusrol, New Jersey. On the Sunday morning he flew from Heathrow, London, to Kennedy, New York, and shared a cab into Manhattan, or so he thought. It turned out that the cab driver, a Russian emigré, was having his first day at the job, and he had no idea where Manhattan was in relation to Kennedy Airport. The next thing he knew, Brian was in the Long Island holiday traffic, and by the time the confused driver finally deposited him in the centre of New York it was nearly four o'clock. Nicklaus was by now half-way through his final round, and in the lead. Brian, in desperation, raced to the helipad and hired a helicopter to take him over the Hudson River to New Jersey. From there, an off-duty air traffic controller who was mercifully a keen golf fan rushed him to Baltusrol in a van. Hardly pausing to collect his credentials, Brian raced on to the course and set off in hot pursuit of Nicklaus. He caught up with him half-way down the 16th fairway, and by the 17th green he had got his breath back and could hold a camera steady. The result is shown on pages 22 and 23.

Over the closing holes of the 1982 US Open at Pebble Beach, Lawrence Levy was in two minds as to where he should be.

He was photographing Tom Watson's attempt at a birdie putt on the 15th green, when the scoreboard indicated that Jack Nicklaus was about to begin the 18th, level with Watson. The 18th was a par five, so Nicklaus would have a birdie chance, and Lawrence decided to let Watson's putt settle the matter. If Watson made it, to go into the lead, Lawrence would stay with him and leave Nicklaus to the photographers already at the 18th. If not, he would join them. Watson missed, so Lawrence ran at full speed the best part of a mile and got there to find Nicklaus safely on the green, but he failed to get his birdie.

What followed was the most inspired action of Lawrence's career. He ran back up the 18th fairway (over 500 yards) and arrived alone at the 17th green just as Watson was leaving the 17th tee, with a horde of photographers behind him. The tee-shot left Watson in a dreadful position, but Lawrence was now in perfect position for his second shot. And anything might happen. The rest is history.

Opposite: Lawrence Levy and a kilted Brian Morgan pose on Swilcan Bridge at the Old Course, St Andrews, with the R and A clubhouse in the background. Above left: Brian always wears a kilt on the final day of the tournament, on this occasion with Lawrence during the 1985 US PGA Championship, at Cherry Hills, Denver. This was the meeting place for somewhat younger workers at the event. Top centre: Lawrence in the long grass at Royal St George's. Above right: Brian sets up a shot with Sandy Lyle and the Open trophy after Sandy's victory in 1985. Above: Lawrence finally receives recognition for his golfing achievements and is congratulated by Greg and Laura Norman with the Open Trophy in 1986 – the year many people think Norman won the title

Severiano Ballesteros

The Champions

There have been many marvellous champions over the past decade or so, all of them worthy of picture profiles. It is bound to appear somewhat arbitrary to illustrate some and not all, but a choice had to be made. In a number of cases it was the easiest thing in the world to do. Who could possibly dream of leaving out Jack Nicklaus or Seve Ballesteros, to name but two?

In some cases the nature of the photographs themselves was a deciding factor. However, we also wanted the choice to reflect the fact that the geographical balance of golfing power is now in flux. European golfers have come very much to the fore in recent years. And, closest to home, it is simply a fact that British golfers have won two of the past three Open Championships. Add Seve Ballesteros and Greg Norman (1984 and 1986) and it begins to seem a fair time since an American raised the Open trophy.

Champions they all are. All of them are interesting, many-sided men as well as outstanding golfers. This is deliberately reflected in the choice of photographs. Lee Trevino clowning like a silent movie comedian – although 'silent' is hardly a word anyone would associate with Super Mex – Bernhard Langer toppling backwards like a felled tree, Greg Norman playing with his delighted daughter in the swimming pool. And so on. Portraits of players and men who have made modern golf the wonderful game it is.

Jack Nicklaus

Bernhard Langer

Arnold Palmer

Sandy Lyle

Tom Watson

Nick Faldo

Lee Trevino

Gary Player

Greg Norman

Raymond Floyd

11

Severiano Ballesteros

There has never been a more exciting golfer than Severiano Ballesteros. Perhaps dramatic is the better word. Sometimes he is the brooding introvert, the tormented genius. At other times the swashbuckling swordsman, with a positively piratical glint in his eye. At all times a driven man – driven by a quest for golfing perfection that borders on the obsessional. Whether or not he is the best golfer of his time, he knows he *should* be, and it is this sense of a man battling with his destiny that gives his game its electrifying quality. Seve Ballesteros is simply thrilling to watch.

He was born in 1957 in Pedrena, Spain, and like many top professionals he showed a precocious talent for the game. He began winning tournaments while still in his teens, and at St Andrews in 1979 he became at 22 the youngest ever winner of the Open Championship. By the end of the 1986 season he had won 50 tournaments worldwide including a second Open, two US Masters and four Suntory World Match Play Championships. In 1986 he won the Epson Order of Merit for the fourth time. He is the outstanding European golfer of the modern era. It is now routine to consider him favourite wherever he chooses to play.

Left: Ballesteros triumphant in front of the Royal and Ancient clubhouse at St Andrews in 1984. His second Open title, following his second victory in the 1983 US Masters, clinched his position at the summit of the golfing world

Top right: In 1979 Ballesteros became the youngest-ever winner of the Open Championship at the age of 22. The scene on the 72nd hole at Royal Lytham and St Annes was filled with emotion, as Seve's brother Baldomero embraced the new champion

Centre: On the eve of the 1984 Open, Ballesteros promised to provide 10 electric-powered wheelchairs for handicapped children if he won. He was obviously delighted to make good his generous offer

Below: His father Baldomero's death in 1986 sadly marred another tremendously successful year for the peerless Spaniard

It feels rather good to hole the best putt of your career in glorious weather on the 72nd at St Andrews – especially when the reward is the Open title. An Open victory is a great achievement at any time, but to win the Open at St Andrews, the home of golf, is very special. Seve's golden moment in 1984 was a nightmare for defending champion Tom Watson, in dire trouble one hole behind

Below: The 19-year-old Ballesteros at Royal Birkdale in 1976, where he finished runner-up to Johnny Miller. That familiar swashbuckling style was already his trademark, as was his extraordinary ability to play aggressively from impossible positions (right) on his way to a second successive victory in the Peugeot French Open

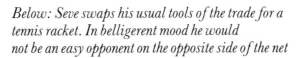

Below: Seve swaps his usual tools of the trade for a tennis racket. In belligerent mood he would not be an easy opponent on the opposite side of the net

Left: Seve's caddie and brother, Vincente, is fairly stricken by this near miss on the 34th green of the 1984 Suntory Match Play final. In fact there was no cause for panic. Seve went on to defeat Bernhard Langer and claim his third Suntory title. Above: Seve stalks the green at Royal St George's in 1985. There is a ferocity about the way in which he is able to concentrate, almost as though he believes he can bend the course to his will

Above: Seve puts the impertinent photographer firmly in his place. Mean and moody he can certainly be, but there is a playful, even impish side to this most fiercely competitive man

Jack Nicklaus

Jack Nicklaus is the greatest champion the game of golf has seen. Indeed, he would be on anyone's shortlist for the title of outstanding sportsman of the 20th century. He has won 20 major championships across a span of three decades, and it is by no means inconceivable that he will add to this total in the future.

As well as being in a class of his own in pure golfing terms, Jack is known worldwide – and by his rivals – for his sportsmanship. The 'Golden Bear' is a great gentleman of the game he has graced for so long. No sport could ask for a finer ambassador.

Nicklaus was born in Columbus, Ohio, in 1940. He won two US Amateur Championships before joining the PGA Tour in 1962. In that year he began his unrivalled record in the majors, winning the US Open. Between then and 1986 he won six US Masters, three Open Championships, three more US Opens and six US PGAs. He has been a member of six Ryder Cup teams, and captained the 1983 team. He did so again in 1987, at the course he designed himself and named Muirfield Village after the Muirfield course where he won his first Open championship.

Jack played the last 10 holes of the 1986 US Masters in seven under par, to win by one stroke. It was the most devastating reply imaginable to those who were foolish enough to regard him as yesterday's man. Many consider this to have been his and the game's most memorable performance.

Left: Nicklaus was visibly affected by the tumultuous applause as he made his way towards the presentation podium at the R and A in 1978. Victory at St Andrews brought him his third Open title – and who would be reckless enough to venture that a fourth remains beyond his grasp?

Above: Nicklaus with his wife, Barbara, and daughter, Nan. Jack enjoys near-regal status in the game of golf, and beyond. During the 1984 Open Championship at St Andrews, he was awarded an honorary degree by the University

Right: Everyone knows that Jack is the greatest of winners, but he has also finished runner-up in more tournaments than any other player. Here he hands over his second-place cheque to Barbara at the conclusion of the 1983 US PGA Championship at the Riviera Country Club, Los Angeles

At the 71st hole of the 1980 US Open, Jack came to the green one shot in the lead over his playing partner, Isao Aoki. Aoki was looking at an eight-footer for a birdie, which in fact he made, while Nicklaus faced this 20-footer for his birdie (far left). The sequence of photographs leaves no doubt about the outcome of that pressure putt – and Nicklaus held on to win the title by that crucial one-stroke margin

Right: In 1984, Jack took part in a four-handed 'skins' game at Phoenix, Arizona. The term 'skin' refers to winning outright on each hole before the skin is awarded. If not, that skin is rolled forward to the next hole, and so on until someone wins a hole. On this occasion, the skin was $10,000 a hole for the first six holes, $20,000 for the next six, and $30,000 for the final six. By the time they reached the 18th, the accumulated skin was a staggering $240,000. Nicklaus chose that moment to strike, sinking the most lucrative single putt in the history of the game

*Above: A 1987 Nicklaus airshot – by Barbara, not Jack, at the Tour Wives Golf Classic
at the Ponte Vedra Club in Jacksonville, Florida. Barbara watches for a
reaction from her husband and Raymond Floyd, the most sympathetic of caddies.
Right: The Nicklaus clan in competition: Jack, with his three sons on the left. From
left to right, Jack Junior, Steve and Gary playing in the Chrysler Team
Championship in Boca Raton, Florida. Jack and Jack Junior were the professionals
while Steve and Gary made up the Pro-Am partnerships*

THRU 14

| LYLE | 2 |
| NICKLAUS | 5 |

4	WATSO
2	PAVIN
0	HAAS. J.
2	McCUMB

NICKLAUS

Two memorable moments in a great career, one in victory, the other in defeat. Right: Jack's wonderful eagle putt at the 15th, during the final round of the 1986 Masters. As he addressed the ball he stood five under par, four strokes behind Seve Ballesteros who was standing on the hill behind, waiting to play his second to the green. The eagle took Nicklaus to seven under, while Ballesteros found the water and fell back to eight under. Birdies at 16 and 17 sent Jack to the clubhouse at nine under, leaving a devastated field in his wake. This was his sixth triumph at Augusta, and it ranks as one of the greatest achievements in the history of the game

Left: Nicklaus walks off the final hole at Turnberry at the conclusion of the 1977 Open Championship – arm in arm with his conqueror, Tom Watson. They had annihilated the rest of the field that day, arriving at the 18th with Watson one stroke in the lead over his playing partner. After two shots Watson was within three feet, Nicklaus a good 40 feet from the pin. The crowd erupted when Nicklaus holed that monstrous birdie putt, leaving Watson suddenly needing his birdie for the Championship. He made it, ending one of the most gripping hand-to-hand confrontations ever witnessed. For Nicklaus, who had fought so hard and played so well, this was surely his finest moment as a sportsman to be so gracious in defeat

27

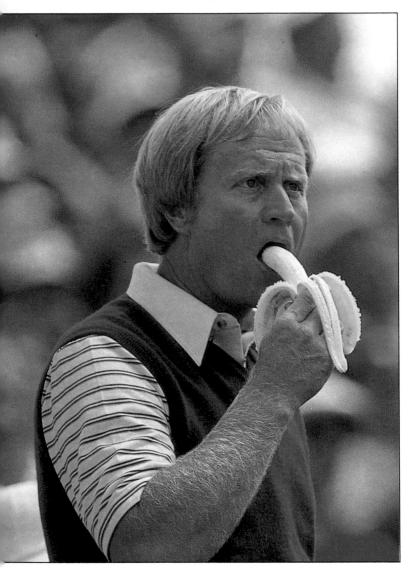

*Above: In recent years, Jack has developed a
passion for bananas, which he can often be
seen consuming between rounds. Apparently
he prizes their potassium content*

*Below: Despite its location, the Bay Hill
Classic at Orlando, Florida,
is not always played in balmy weather.
Jack is deep in contemplation, comforted
by an oversize pair of warming gloves*

*Above: At a Pro-Am organized by his wife
Barbara for the Fellowship of Christian
Athletes at Loxahatchee, Palm Beach,
Florida, the 'Golden Bear' displays his new
mascot in the form of a head-cover*

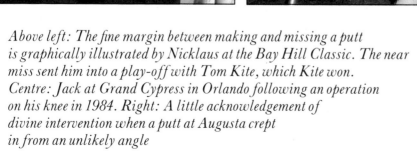

Above left: The fine margin between making and missing a putt is graphically illustrated by Nicklaus at the Bay Hill Classic. The near miss sent him into a play-off with Tom Kite, which Kite won. Centre: Jack at Grand Cypress in Orlando following an operation on his knee in 1984. Right: A little acknowledgement of divine intervention when a putt at Augusta crept in from an unlikely angle

Tom Watson

Tom Watson has often been described as an all-American boy, in the best sense of that phrase – modest of manner, unfailingly courteous and uncomplaining in adversity. He is indeed that, but he is also one of the most aggressive players in the game. And he is one of the greatest champions of the modern era. Watson would dearly like to win a sixth Open to equal Harry Vardon's record.

In the mid-1980s, Watson's form began to elude him, mainly because his aggressive putting style was bound to punish mistakes harshly. The 1987 US Open and Open Championships saw him firmly back in contention, however, and there is every reason to believe that victories will come his way again.

Watson was born in Kansas City, Missouri, in 1949. He turned professional in 1971, and scored the first of his remarkable run of victories in the Open Championship at Carnoustie in 1975. As well as five Open titles, he has twice won the US Masters and once the US Open – the latter on the strength of an astonishing shot on the 71st hole. He has five times been the leading money winner on the PGA Tour, and in terms of career earnings he ranks second only to Nicklaus.

Left: Watson acknowledges the cheers of the crowd, following the conclusive putt on the 72nd at Muirfield to win his third Open Championship in 1980

Above right: Tom has good reason for displaying pro-Scottish sentiments, following his fourth Open success on Scottish soil at Royal Troon in 1982. Below: Linda Watson shares her husband's triumph at Muirfield in 1980

As the 1982 US Open at Pebble Beach reached its climax,
Watson and Nicklaus were level. Jack was beside the 18th green,
watching on television, as Tom languished in the semi-rough
on the par three 17th. From that lie, his chances of getting up
and down in two were minimal. Watson simply chipped in for
a miraculous birdie. Then he birdied the 18th for good measure,
and fell delightedly into his caddie's arms

*Above: As at Turnberry in 1977, one gallant
sportsman congratulates another. Nicklaus acknowledges
Watson's stunning display over the last two
holes of the 1982 US Open at Pebble Beach.
For all his many titles, this was Tom's first
success in his national championship*

*Above left: In the course of his career, Watson has taken a great deal
of advice and technical instruction from Byron Nelson, here with Tom at Augusta.
Centre: During the 1985 Open
at Royal St George's, Tom found himself in the long grass.
Right: A happier misfortune befell him at
Royal Birkdale in 1983, when he dropped the winner's trophy and
cheerfully displayed the result to the cameras*

Greg Norman

Greg Norman had an extraordinary year in 1986. He topped the US prize-money list and won the Open Championship by a commanding five strokes. And those achievements must be viewed in the light of what he *nearly* achieved. He led going into the final rounds of both the US Masters and US Open, but victory escaped him. Then, after winning the Open, he found himself again in the leading position going into the final round of the US PGA – for the fourth time in the four majors. Bob Tway and Lady Luck then took a hand, and of course she would team up with Larry Mize a few months later in the US Masters.

If Norman had actually won everything in sight, as he threatened to do, the golfing world would surely have trembled. As it was, the powerful Australian took his promised place at the top table reserved for the golfing élite. The 'Great White Shark' is everybody's bet to remain there for a long time – and more major titles will undoubtedly fall before him.

Norman was born in Queensland in 1955, and took up the game at the comparatively late age of 16. He turned professional in 1976, and during the next decade won 41 tournaments worldwide. In 1982 he won the European Order of Merit, and on three occasions he has won the Suntory World Match Play Championship.

Opposite: Norman tees off on the ninth hole, Bruce's Castle, at Turnberry on his way to the 1986 Open title. The lighthouse looms in the background. Right: A jubilant Norman during his second round 63 at Turnberry in the 1986 Open Championship. This tied the course record, and had he not three-putted in the 18th he would have established a championship record as well. With that spectacular round behind him, Greg went on to victory by a comfortable five-stroke margin

Far left: The way the course was set up by the R and A for the 1986 Open at Turnberry, with extremely narrow fairways, brought the rough very much into play. Greg plays out of it on the uphill seventh hole. Left: During the first round, he found himself playing out of the long grass by the 14th fairway. Right: The final putt on the 72nd, and Greg prepares to embrace his caddie, Pete Bender. Above right: With his wife, Laura, and the coveted Open trophy. Far right: Greg and friends celebrate the Turnberry victory at midnight on the 18th green

Above: The final round of the 1987 US Masters dealt Norman one of golf's most cruel blows. After making a great putt at the 17th to draw level with Seve Ballesteros and Larry Mize, he narrowly missed a putt at the 18th that would have given him outright victory (right). The scene was now set for Larry Mize to pull off the most audacious of chip shots to win the sudden-death play-off

Left: The anguish of a missed putt during the 1986 US PGA Championship at Toledo, Ohio. Greg had victory here snatched from his grasp, when Bob Tway spectacularly holed out from the bunker on the final hole. Above: The 1984 US Open at Winged Foot, New York, saw Greg hole a momentous 40-foot putt from the edge of the green on to the 72nd, to tie Fuzzy Zoeller. But Zoeller won the play-off

*Left: Greg the hunter during
a fishing and camping excursion to
Australia's Fraser Island, the largest
sand island in the world. American-based,
Norman makes frequent visits
to his native Australia.
Above left: At the 1986 Ford Classic in
Paris, Greg won his weight in
champagne for recording the lowest score
of the day. Above right: Norman urges on his
team-mate, David Graham, during the
inaugural Dunhill Nations Cup at
St Andrews in 1985. With Graham Marsh
completing the side, the Australians emerged
victorious. Below left: The 'Great White Shark'
holds no terrors for his daughter, Morgan-Leigh,
as they splash in the pool at home in
Orlando, Florida. Below right: Norman was
characteristically gracious in defeat after
Fuzzy Zoeller beat him in the play-off
for the 1984 US Open Championship*

Bernhard Langer

Bernhard Langer was a well-established star on the European circuit when he won the US Masters in 1985. This cool, meticulous stroke-maker had emerged as Seve Ballesteros's greatest European rival, and like the Spaniard he now starts any tournament anywhere at short odds.

Langer is an exceptionally gifted iron-player, and where once he had a nightmarish time with short putts, today he putts cross-handed, and consistently as well as anyone. He joined the American PGA Tour in 1985, and unlike Ballesteros he shows no reluctance to follow that particular trail. Along with Greg Norman and Ballesteros, it is Langer who has most forcibly reminded the Americans that they can no longer count on having things their own way, even on home ground.

Bernhard Langer was born in Anhausen, West Germany, in 1957. He started caddying at a tender age, but his ambition was always to play and he turned professional at the age of 15. By the end of 1986 he had won 24 international tournaments, including four German Opens, two Irish Opens and one French, Spanish and Dutch Open. He has been a member of three Ryder Cup teams, including the Victorious 1985 Squad and in 1981 and 1984 he won the European Order of Merit.

Left: Seve Ballesteros hardly shares his elation as Langer holes a birdie putt on the 71st at Augusta in 1985. Right: Bernhard went on to win the Masters by a two-stroke margin, and was presented with the coveted green jacket by the defending champion, Ben Crenshaw

Right: Langer invokes the gods after missing an eagle putt on the 15th at Augusta during the final round of the 1985 US Masters. But a final birdie at the 17th saw him safely to victory. Far right: A missed putt at the final hole of the 1983 Johnnie Walker Tournament at Madrid saw Bernhard in more restrained despair. Again, he won the tournament

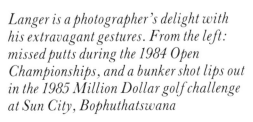

Langer is a photographer's delight with his extravagant gestures. From the left: missed putts during the 1984 Open Championships, and a bunker shot lips out in the 1985 Million Dollar golf challenge at Sun City, Bophuthatswana

*Above right: Langer gets the measure
of the Augusta National before his successful
assault on the 1985 Masters.
Below right: Bernhard
looks somewhat taken aback to discover
a stranger on the green during the
1984 Carrolls Irish Open, which he won.
The Royal Dublin course is a
conservation area for wildlife, which
means the hares are shooed out of
the back gate early in the morning and let
back in at night when play has finished.
This one obviously missed reveille*

*Like many top players, Langer
works at the technical aspects of
his game with a trusted friend and
mentor. Above left: Willie Hoffman
caddied for Bernhard at the 1986
US Open at Shinnecock Hills,
New York. Below left: Langer was
competing against Ballesteros in the
final of the Suntory World Match
Play Championship at Wentworth
in 1984, when on the par five
fourth hole he hit his drive into a
bush. Even from there he is
prepared to attack with a wood, the
sort of aggressive play that
matchplay encourages. But Seve went
on to win – and repeated his victory
over Bernhard the following year.
Left: Langer holes a putt on
the final green in the 1981
Benson & Hedges
International Open.
He went on that year to top
the European Order of Merit for
the first time*

Lee Trevino

Lee Trevino enjoys a unique position in the affections of a generation of golf fans. He emerged from obscurity to win the 1968 US Open Championship, and no one could recall seeing a golfer from a similar mould. 'Super Mex', as the stocky little Texas-born Mexican was affectionately named, appeared to be unorthodox in every way. He seemed to strike the ball in an oddly flat manner, and yet he possessed a bewildering array of strokes. And there was that incessant chattering and wise-cracking between shots that became his indelible trademark.

Much of the Trevino myth is simply that – myth. That swing, for example, may look eccentric to the layman but it is really quite beautifully fashioned. Expert observers claim that it allows him to keep the club face square through the hitting area marginally longer than normal, which increases his control. This in turn permits him to play all those deft little touch shots which so delight his fans. As for the chattering, his opponents will tell you that it has never affected Trevino's concentration. He simply has the ability to switch his concentration on and off like an electric light. He enters a completely private world as he squares up for his shot – and indeed he is regarded as a very private man, in contrast to his flamboyant public image.

Trevino was born in Dallas in 1939. He openly admits to having been a golf hustler in his early years, but since he joined the PGA Tour in 1968 there has been nothing calculated about his efforts. He has twice won the Open Championship, twice the US Open and twice the US PGA Championship.

Contrasting moods. Left: Trevino ponders a putt at Shinnecock Hills during the 1986 US Open. Right: A laughing Lee savours his nation's victory in the 1979 Ryder Cup at The Greenbrier, West Virginia. This was the first occasion on which the Americans faced a European rather than a British challenge

Above: Trevino at the Phoenix Open in 1982 under the watchful eye not only of his long-serving caddie, Herman Mitchell, but of an armed guard as well. He had received a threat to his life. Right: Lee in the heavy rough at Royal Birkdale in 1983, scene of the first of his two successive Open Championships in 1971

Far left: Textbook steadiness of the head as Lee competes in the Tournament Players Championship at Sawgrass, Florida. He won the tournament in 1980. Left: The following year, Trevino contested a special charity match in company with the reigning title holders of the majors.
Tom Watson currently held the Open title, Jack Nicklaus the US Open and PGA and Seve Ballesteros the US Masters

*Above: Trevino's flat swing, with the rounded finish, is recognizable
from two fairways away. Golf teachers have long realized
that there is nothing quirky about it. In fact,
it allows him longer than normal extension through the ball.
In other words, his clubhead stays square a fraction longer in the
vital hitting area. In theory, this gives him
the advantage of greater control*

*Above left: Trevino has immense respect for the traditions of the game.
During the 1984 Open Championship at St Andrews, he was filmed discussing the finer points of his
swing with Laurie Auchterlonie, last clubmaker in the honourable tradition
of fashioning wooden clubs by hand. Laurie's father won the Open Championship in 1893.
Below left: Lee poses with the late Joan Ryder-Scarfe, the daughter of
Sam Ryder who founded the Ryder Cup competition. Above right: Trevino the exuberant
TV commentator for NBC, and below right: getting a bit of his own brand of teasing from Isao Aoki*

Arnold Palmer

Professional golf is deeply indebted to Arnold Palmer. He emerged in the 1950s as a dynamic new force in the game, an aggressive player – and especially putter – who managed to convey to a wider public the sheer exhilaration of striking a golf ball. 'Arnie's Army' was born, and he remains hugely popular everywhere in the world.

Britain has particular reason to venerate Palmer. In 1960 he announced his intention of coming over for the Open Championship at St Andrews. He lost to the Australian Kel Nagle, but he won the Open title the following two years. Palmer's commitment to the Open Championship re-established it as a truly international competition. The rising generation of American stars followed Palmer, and for many of them the winning of the Open Championship became the summit of ambition. In tacit recognition of Palmer's invaluable contribution to the sport, the R and A have amended the rules of entry so that Palmer, and any other ex-champion, can now compete in the Open until the age of 65.

As a former Masters winner, Arnold is entitled to play the tournament for life. The PGA of America honoured him with a lifetime exemption to their championship in 1984, despite the fact he has never won the event. It is a pity that the US Golf Association has failed to make a similar gesture towards the father of modern golf.

Arnold Palmer was born in Latrobe, Pennsylvania, in 1929. He turned professional after winning the 1954 US Amateur Championship. Along with his two Open titles he has won 61 tournaments on the PGA Tour, including four US Masters and the US Open. As a charter member of the Senior PGA Tour he continues to delight several generations of his legions of fans.

Left: Palmer's high finish is characteristic of his swing. So too is the way he follows the flight of the ball with the club extended in front of him, sometimes using his body to twist and turn the club. Right: On the 14th tee at the Tournament Players Club, Arnold displays his driving technique

*Below: The closing stages of the first round
of the 1983 US Masters found Palmer in serious contention.
Birdies at the 15th and 16th left him just one shot off the pace.
This 45-footer on the 17th hole would have given him his
vital birdie. The slump of dejection tells the result*

Above: The grittiest of competitors, even in middle age, Palmer blasts his way out of a bunker at the 10th hole at Augusta during the 1983 US Masters

Below: The tournament host is having bunker trouble at the 1981 Bay Hill Classic. Palmer's last tour win was in 1973, but he remains a formidable competitor on the Seniors circuit

Right: Not a dance of the matadors, but an unsuccessful attempt to force a putt into the hole by using body language at Bear Creek, Southern California, in 1985

The moods of an old warrior in adversity. Far left: Head down in despair after missing the second green at the Augusta National par three tournament. Left: Seething with anger at himself after missing a putt at the 1981 Bay Hill Classic

Above: Palmer watches a putt slide by the hole during the 1983 US Open at Oakmont, Pennsylvania

Right: Palmer and a group of friends had just set a new record for circling the globe by executive jet. Hawker Siddeley, recognizing the aviation achievement, were happy to give him the opportunity to savour the delights of a rare Tiger Moth. Below: At the end of a day's work at the Bay Hill Club, Orlando, Arnold sets off behind the wheel of his golf cart, a special reproduction of the red tractor he uses in television advertisements for an oil company

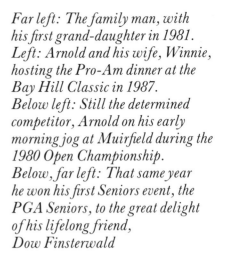

Far left: The family man, with his first grand-daughter in 1981.
Left: Arnold and his wife, Winnie, hosting the Pro-Am dinner at the Bay Hill Classic in 1987.
Below left: Still the determined competitor, Arnold on his early morning jog at Muirfield during the 1980 Open Championship.
Below, far left: That same year he won his first Seniors event, the PGA Seniors, to the great delight of his lifelong friend, Dow Finsterwald

Gary Player

Gary Player has, in global terms, an unequalled record. He has played more and won more in more places than any golfer in history, and it is not surprising that he claims to have travelled more miles than any other sportsman. He is in the select company of Gene Sarazen, Ben Hogan and Jack Nicklaus as one of only four grand slam winners – the four major titles. And he is the only player ever to win the Open Championship in three consecutive decades – 1959, 1968 and 1974.

Player has never made any secret about the reasons for his phenomenal success. Some would consider his unquenchable thirst for victory fanatical, but Gary argues that it is simply a matter of total professionalism. He is certainly committed to golfing excellence, as he is to physical fitness and, above all, to the power of positive thinking. Some of his attitudes may be very individual, but everyone should copy the way he blasts out of a bunker. He is the finest sand player in living memory.

Gary Player was born in Johannesburg in 1935. He turned professional in 1953, and since then he has claimed well over 100 tournament victories. These include three Open Championships, three US Masters, two US PGA and one US Open. He has won the World Match Play Championship five times, and continues to compete at an international and Senior level.

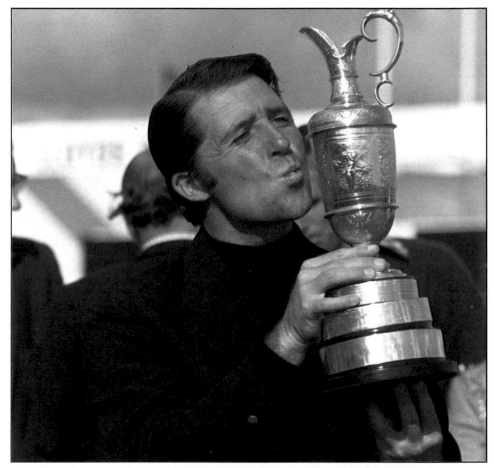

Left: A light-hearted moment as Gary's hat blows away, but this steeliest of sportsmen is anything but light-hearted in his approach to his profession. Above right: He kisses the trophy at Royal Lytham and St Annes in 1974, the scene of his third Open victory. Below right: Player's fitness is legendary, and his record in major championships stamps him as an all-time great

Above: Gary's mood seems not to match his cheery attire, as he
communes with himself during the 1980 South African Open.
He failed to capture his national title on this occasion, but he has
won it a phenomenal 13 times since 1956

Left: Player at the 1984 Suntory World Match Play Championship at Wentworth, the 21st anniversary of the competition. Seve Ballesteros won the title that year, but with five victories Player remains the most successful competitor to date. Above: Player missed a putt during the 1979 US Open Championship at the Inverness Club, Toledo, Ohio. He finished in a tie for second place behind Hale Irwin

Above: The veteran contender in happy mood before teeing off for the 1983 Open Championship at Royal Birkdale. Above right: Typically, Gary was the last player out on the practice ground at Augusta before the 1982 Masters. Late into a rainy evening his son, Wayne, uses a club to hold his head still. Below right: Player demonstrates the extraordinary strength of his fingers. It is difficult enough to hold one club the way he is holding two

Far left: During the searing heat of the 1981 US PGA Championship at the Atlantic Athletic Club, Georgia, Gary resorted to throwing cold water over himself to keep cool. Above: Gary and his son, Wayne, at a Press Conference during the 1982 US Open. Wayne had qualified to play – the first time a father and son had achieved this distinction. Left: Gary with his wife, Vivien, who mostly stays at home in South Africa, running their farm and bringing up their five children

Sandy Lyle

In 1985 Scotland's Sandy Lyle became the first home winner of the Open Championship since Tony Jacklin in 1969. In that memorable year Lyle helped Europe to regain the Ryder Cup trophy for the first time in 28 years, and he won the European Order of Merit as Europe's leading money-winner.

Lyle is an unassuming man, on and off the course, and he seems to be utterly absorbed by golf. His uncomplicated nature, however, may be a source of strength as a player. He won his Open title by playing with great self-possession over the final holes, while all around him were succumbing to the pressure of the occasion. His ability to cope with pressure is an enviable attribute, and it means that whenever he finds himself in contention and playing well, he is quite likely to slide past the winning post, like a horse coming unnoticed along the rails. It is idle to speculate on combined characteristics, but a blend of Sandy's cool and Seve's fire would be awesome.

Sandy Lyle was born in Shrewsbury in 1958 of Scottish parents. He has been a member of four Ryder Cup teams, and three times won the European Order of Merit. In 1987 he was awarded the MBE for his golfing achievements, and won the Tournament Players Championship in Jacksonville, Florida.

Left: Lyle's victory in the 1985 Open Championship at Royal St George's was the first by a British player since Tony Jacklin's memorable win in 1969. Right: Sandy was presented not only with the trophy, but also with the Tom Morris belt in recognition of this proud day for one of Scotland's sons

Left: A sequence showing the vital putt of Sandy Lyle's final round of the 1985 Open Championship. Following a birdie at the 14th, this 18-foot putt on the 15th gave him the breathing space he needed for the final run in to victory. Right: Not even a fluffed chip shot on the 18th could prevent him from carrying off his first Open trophy

Above: The future Open champion practising at the Augusta National before the 1981 US Masters. His father and coach, Alex, casts a critical eye on his protégé's swing.
Right: Rain forces a smiling Sandy to take shelter under an umbrella with his long-serving caddie and friend, Dave Musgrove.
Far right: Sandy looks to the heavens after holing a putt at the 1987 Tournament Players Championship at Jacksonville Beach, Florida. He went on to win the tournament, the first British player ever to do so. Victory brought him an automatic 10-year exemption from qualifying for the US PGA Tour

Below: The photographer is immortalized in the Lyle family video album during the christening celebrations for Sandy's son, James, at his Wentworth home in 1986

Above: Sandy leaps for joy after holing a critical putt at the 34th in the final of the 1982 Suntory World Match Play Championship at Wentworth. This putt kept alive his hopes of becoming the first British winner, but he was eventually beaten by Seve Ballesteros at the first hole of the sudden-death play-off

Above: Lyle talks to the world's press after his victory in the 1987 Tournament Players Championship. Delighted as he was, Sandy kept things in perspective. When asked by an American reporter what he thought was the difference between this tournament and the Open Championship in terms of prestige, Sandy simply replied, 'About 120 years.'

Raymond Floyd

Every year, Raymond Floyd tees off in the Open Championship knowing he is only 72 holes away from becoming the fifth man ever to win the grand slam. He has been such a good golfer for such a long time that it will be highly appropriate if he achieves his dream.

Floyd is a stylish man both on and off the course. In his younger days he enjoyed a reputation as a hell-raiser, but now he takes his pleasures in a more subdued fashion. He is popular, partly because he has a way of confounding both his critics and the advancing years. Whenever it seems his distinguished career is finally on the wane, that is precisely when he is most likely to strike. In recent years he seems to have become an even more impressive player than he was in his supposed prime. And in coming from behind to win the 1986 US Open at Shinnecock Hills, New York, he became the oldest-ever winner of that title. When will Raymond finally claim his Open Championship?

Raymond Floyd was born in 1942 in North Carolina. He joined the PGA Tour in 1963, and by the end of 1986 he had amassed a total of 21 Tour victories. He has won the US Masters, the US Open, and twice the US PGA Championship.

Above left: Raymond with his wife, Maria, and daughter, Christina, after being presented with the trophy for winning the US Open Championship at Shinnecock Hills in 1986. At the age of 43 he became the oldest winner of the tournament. Below left: A kiss from his wife during the 1985 Ryder Cup competition at The Belfry

Far left: Floyd disconsolate after missing a putt during the 1985 US Masters. Left: In rather jollier mood, Raymond throws his visor in the air after holing a crucial putt at the 1982 Sun City Million Dollar Golf Challenge, Bophuthatswana. He won the $300,000 first prize, the winner's biggest cheque in golf

Right: During the Sun City Million Dollar Golf Challenge, Raymond is given some help for a painful back by his caddie, whose own back must be made of iron. Far right: The resilient Floyd protects himself from the elements during the 1986 Open Championship at Turnberry

Above: Raymond proves that fitness is essential to championship golf as he tunes up for the 1978 Open at St Andrews. Left: Raymond, practising in Florida, looks as if he is aiming for the pot of gold at the end of the rainbow

Nick Faldo

From his earliest days as an amateur, much has been expected of Nick Faldo, not least by himself. Through the mid-1980s, however, it seemed that his immense promise might stop short of being truly fulfilled. His victory in the 1987 Open Championship at Muirfield must be all the sweeter because it is a vindication of his unwavering faith in himself.

If Faldo goes on from triumph to triumph, the turning point in his career will have been his decision in 1984 to change his swing. He did this against a lot of advice, because his easy, elegant swing had long been admired. Nick, however, saw it differently. He believed that it was too loose, lazy even, to hold up under the pressure of trying to win a major championship on the final day. So he put himself in the skilled hands of English golf teacher Dave Leadbetter in Florida, remodelled his swing and suffered a couple of dreadful seasons while he adjusted to it. The result was plain for all to see at Muirfield – the final 18 holes were played in absolutely strict par, hole by hole, in spite of awful weather conditions.

Nick Faldo was born in Welwyn Garden City in 1957. He was outstanding as a teenager, winning the British Youth's Open Amateur Championship and the English Amateur Championship in 1975. He turned professional the following year, and since then he has won the Sea Pines Heritage Classic on the American Tour, three European PGA championships, and several other European Tour events including four consecutive tournaments in 1983. Nick has been a member of six Ryder Cup teams, and in 1983 he won the European Order of Merit.

Left: Having holed his putt on the final hole of the 1987 Open Championship at Muirfield, Faldo raises his arms in triumph. He then went straight to the clubhouse, without even glancing at the scoreboard to see how Paul Azinger was faring at the 17th. Right: The new Open Champion with the coveted trophy

Nick calls this comic routine 'the leather mashie'. He follows an air shot through with his right foot – on this occasion with mock-horrific consequences

*Above: To launch the Sea Pines Heritage Classic at Harbour Town, South Carolina,
the defending champion, dressed in a tartan jacket, drives the ball into
the Calibogue Sound. He does so to the accompaniment
of a thunderous cannon shot. Having won this tournament in 1984,
Nick had to suffer this ordeal the following year. Right: Fatherhood obviously sits
well with Faldo, as he happily protects himself from the Hawaiian sun
with baby Natalie's bonnet at the Kapalua International*

Hits and Misses

At any level of play golf provides its share of triumphant moments – and, as any golfer knows, far more than its share of terrible disappointments. In the professional game, where there is so much at stake, these high and low points have an added edge. The entire course of a player's career can be determined by making or missing a single putt under the most severe pressure. Even more cruelly, a freakish accident or an opponent's fluke can transform a match in a way that would have seemed quite impossible a split second before.

No-one who watched them on television will ever forget the fate that befell Greg Norman in successive majors. Bob Tway's miraculous bunker shot on the final hole of the 1986 US PGA Championship must have seemed a once-in-a-lifetime nightmare for the Australian star. What on earth would he have thought if he had looked into a crystal ball and seen what Larry Mize would do to him in the 1987 US Masters? Pure serendipity for Tway and Mize, of course, and no-one should begrudge them their good fortune. But they were terrible twin blows for the gallant Norman to endure.

For the most part, golf is an individual competition and its joys and sorrows are solitary. Team competitions add another dimension: shared consolation among the losers, shared triumph for the victors. Was there ever a happier bunch than the European Ryder Cup team at The Belfry in 1985, or the Great Britain and Ireland Curtis Cup team at Prairie Dunes, Kansas, in 1986?

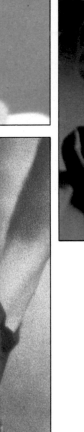

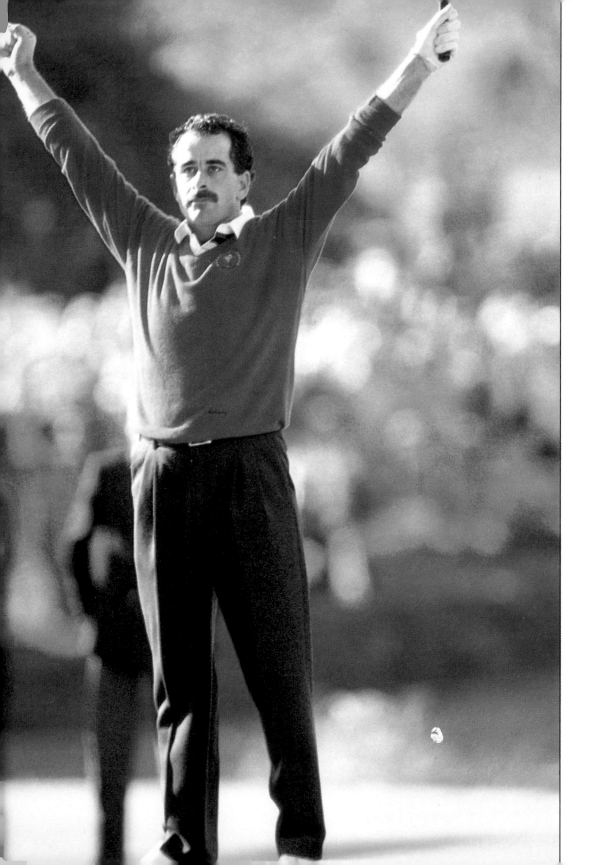

September 15 1985 was a memorable day
in the history of European golf. After 28 years, the
American domination of the Ryder Cup was finally broken. Left:
The moment of victory came when Britain's Sam Torrance holed
a long putt at the 18th to defeat Andy North, and raised his
arms in triumph to an ecstatic crowd. Above: The European
team's jubilation at The Belfry, Sutton Coldfield, was
unrestrained. It is champagne all the way as
Sam Torrance wraps his arms around Paul Way and a grinning
Ian Woosnam. Right: Victorious captain Tony Jacklin is on
top of the world – and literally on top of the roof at
The Belfry, chaired by Torrance. Seve Ballesteros and Paul Way
look on happily as the Jacklin hand and the Howard Clark
flag wave to the crowd

Before 1979 the Ryder Cup Match was contested between the United States and a joint Great Britain and Ireland side, and with rare exceptions the Americans proved too strong. Changing the elegibility rules to include continental golfers was an attempt to raise the level of competition. In 1983 Europe came close to winning at PGA National in Palm Beach Gardens. Two years later at The Belfry the dream came true, and the victory margin was, in the end, quite comfortable. Above: The Spanish quartet played a decisive role. From left to right: José-María Canizares, Seve Ballesteros, Manual Pinero and José Rivero. Nicknamed the 'Spanish Armada', they were more than welcomed to England's shores. Right: Jacklin and the entire winning side enjoy the presentation ceremony outside The Belfry Hotel. Far right: The opposing captains, Tony Jacklin and Lee Trevino. Jacklin, always clutching that portable television set, threw himself into the competition with tremendous gusto; Trevino seemed uncharacterstically subdued throughout

*Left and above: Andy North has never been a big winner despite his
hectic schedule on the US Tour. He has, however, won
two US Opens. On both occasions he had to get up and down from a bunker late
in the round to win by the narrowest of margins. In these
pictures he is seen not only recovering from the deep bunker
on the 17th hole at Oakland Hills during the 1985 Championship,
but playing the shot so well that the ball finished three inches from the hole*

Far left and left: Chen Tze-Chung went into the final round of the 1985 US Open two strokes in the lead over his playing partner, Andy North. On the fifth hole, disaster struck. In the course of making a quadruple bogey eight, he actually suffered the ignominy of a double hit, trying to pitch out of the rough. North went on to win

Above: At the 71st hole of the 1984 Open Championship at St Andrews, Tom Watson tried to play a floating long iron shot on to the top level of the green. He overshot the green and landed up over the road and against the wall. He attempted his recovery shot with his caddie, Alfie Fyles, looking on dejectedly: Ballesteros, meanwhile, birdied 18 to ensure victory. Right: Tom Kite in despair as his putt slides by the final hole to let Jack Nicklaus win the 1986 US Masters

Bob Tway holes out from the bunker on the final hole of the
1986 US PGA Championship at the Inverness Country Club,
Toledo, Ohio. As a consequence, he won the tournament that
a moment before his shot had seemed securely in Greg Norman's
hands. Tway may have had difficulty believing his luck, but he
certainly had no trouble responding to it

Larry Mize at the climax of the 1987 US Masters. He had tied with Seve Ballesteros and Greg Norman after 72 holes, and Ballesteros had dropped out at the first extra hole. At the second, Norman reached the green in two, and was poised for victory: Mize was well short and to the right after his second shot. From that position, few would have given him much chance of getting down in two. The most likely outcome was that he would bogey the hole, leaving Norman to win with a routine par. But the gods had other ideas. Mize chipped straight into the hole, and a devastated Norman could not match miracle with miracle

Left: A delighted Payne Stewart wins the 1987 Bay Hill Classic at Orlando, Florida. He could not have been closer to home, which is adjacent to the 12th tee. Below: Every day on his round he was able to greet his baby daughter, Chelsea, through the railings. Payne donated his entire winner's cheque of $108,000 to cancer research following his father's death the previous year

Left and below: Seve Ballesteros finds the water with his second shot at the 15th hole during the final round of the 1986 US Masters, the result of which was greeted by a momentous cheer from the gallery supporting Nicklaus, who had just eagled the hole and was lining up a birdie putt on the adjacent 16th

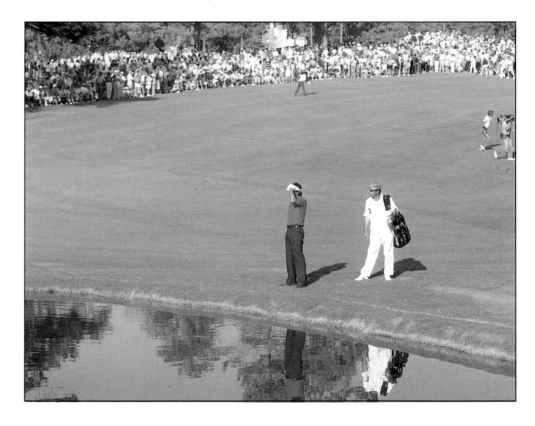

Bitter disappointment for Paul Azinger at the very end of the 1987 Open Championship at Muirfield. Having led throughout most of the tournament, and by three strokes only a few holes before, he needed a par on the 18th hole to tie Nick Faldo. Above: Bunkered after his second shot, he needed to get up and down to tie. Right: The long putt eluded him, and he dropped his putter in dejection

Above: Curtis Strange in dire trouble at Rae's Creek, a fiendish hazard at the 13th hole of the Augusta National, during the final round of the 1985 US Masters. For his second shot he had chosen wood, gambling on being able to carry the water to set up an eagle opportunity. The previous year, Ben Crenshaw had found himself in an identical position. While trying to make up his mind whether to lay up with his second, or to take the gamble, he had spotted among the spectators Billy Jo Patton, a previous victim of Rae's Creek. Taking it as a sign, he had chosen caution and went on to win; Strange paid the penalty for his gamble – and lost

Above: To his caddie's undisguised joy, Ben Crenshaw holes a birdie putt on the 15th hole during the final round of the 1984 US Masters. He went on to win the coveted green jacket. Right: A jubilant Jerry Pate, the winner of the 1981 Tournament Players Championship, threw Deane Beman, the Tour Commissioner, and Pete Dye, the course architect, into the lake beside the 18th green of the Tournament Players Club at Sawgrass. The new course had received unanimous disapproval from the players. Pate then jumped in himself

The Ladies

Like women's tennis, women's golf is not just a pale reflection of the men's game. Women may play with less power, but their game has its own strengths and is no less absorbing. The finest women golfers display the most scintillating iron play, especially in those subtle shots around the green.

Women's amateur golf has always had an enthusiastic following, but the professional game is a relative newcomer. Although today it is a flourishing concern in the United States, the most successful players on the LPGA tour earn sums that would be the envy of some of the men on tour. In 1981 Kathy Whitworth, JoAnne Carner and Donna Caponi all joined the millionaires club, with Nancy Lopez and Pat Bradley following a few years later. Whether amateur or professional, the woman's game can stand alone as an exciting and colourful sport.

In Europe the WPGA has found its feet after the inevitable teething problems they faced at the start in 1979. They have found a star performer in Laura Davies who is the first woman in the history of the game to hold both the US Women's Open and the British Ladies Open and has raised the status at the WPGA as Nancy Lopez did for the LPGA across the water.

With the Great Britain and Ireland Curtis Cup team winning for the first time on American soil in 1986 at Prairie Dunes, Kansas, the ladies of Europe are beginning to show signs of being able to compete against the world in the same way as Seve Ballesteros, Bernhard Langer and Sandy Lyle and the Ryder Cup team of 1985 have for the men.

Left: Nancy Lopez dominated the Women's Tour for several years in the 1970's, not only as a great player but also as a glamorous, fun-loving individual. She has won all of the major ladies titles at least once, and has continued to play despite having two small daughters. In this series of photographs she sinks a long putt during the 1980 World Championship of Women's Golf

Left: JoAnne Carner has for
many years been the
brightest star on the Ladies
circuit. Affectionately known as
'Big Moma' she is one
of the all-time greats
of women's golf. She
had compiled one of the
finest amateur records ever
before turning professional in
1970. Since then she has won
more tournaments and more
money than any other woman.
In victory or defeat,
JoAnne vents her emotions
to the full – and is a
golf photographer's dream.
Here she shows her
understandable delight at holing
a bunker shot on her way
to winning the 1983 World
Championship of Women's Golf

Left: In 1986 Britain and Ireland defeated the United States to win the Curtis Cup for the first time in 30 years. The victorious team members pose with their trophy after winning by a decisive 13 to five margin at Prairie Dunes, Kansas. Above: Jill Thornhill gives Lillian Behan a congratulatory hug

Above: A smiling Captain Diane Bailey looks on as Patricia Johnson receives a handshake. Patricia won the point that ensured victory. Below left: Diane Bailey congratulates her vice-captain, Elsie Brown. Below: Belle Robertson, the senior player of the British and Irish side, grins delightedly

Right: Nancy Lopez took up the game of golf at the age of eight under the guidance of her father, Domingo, pictured with his celebrated daughter in 1979. In 1978, her first year as a professional, Nancy won nine tournaments, five of them in a row, and was named both Rookie of the Year and Player of the Year. Eight tournament victories and a second consecutive Player of the Year award followed in 1979. Far right: The ever stylish Kathy Baker, the 1984 US Women's Open Champion, competing at Sun City, Bophuthatswana

*Above: Nancy Lopez in whimsical mood
while the Australian beauty Jan Stephenson (right)
looks pensive. Jan is very much the
glamour girl of the circuit,
but she is also an exceptionally fine golfer.
She won the 1983 US Women's Open Championship,
and her career earnings to date prove her
to be one of the most successful players*

Right: The engaging Muffin Spencer-Devlin one of the tour's most striking characters as well as a talented golfer. Far right: In 1987 Laura Davies became the first woman ever to hold both the Ladies British Open and the US Women's Open at the same time – albeit only for a week. She had to defend her British title the week immediately following her victory in America and only missed success by one shot. Laura is pictured holding both trophies at St Mellion in Cornwall

Left: Kathy Whitworth at the 1982 CPC Women's International at Moss Creek Plantation, Hilton Head Island, South Carolina, on the way to yet another victory. Kathy has won 88 tournaments on the US LPGA Tour, making her the most successful woman golfer ever. Above: Most women on the US Tour have male caddies. Here Sally Little receives some comfort from hers

On and around the Tour

The professional golf tour has an almost magnetic attraction. Wherever it pitches its tent, the same faces keep popping up. Caddies, of course, but keen spectators, too, seem to be on hand at every possible opportunity. Professional tournament circuits are organized in the United States, Europe, Japan, Australia and New Zealand, Africa, South Africa and the Far East. These events enjoy enthusiastic support.

The major tournaments have a very special flavour, each different from the others. The first of the season, the US Masters, is the only one of the four majors to have a permanent home at Augusta, Georgia. It is an exclusive affair run by the Augusta National Golf Club. Tickets for the Masters are the hardest to come by in the golfing world, and it is a standing joke in Augusta that life-time tickets loom as large as houses in divorce settlements.

The US Open, the second in the season, is run by the United States Golf Association in conjunction with the club chosen for the venue. As a result it is often fraught with organizational difficulties. Nevertheless, the championship carries great prestige among golfers, and it is not surprisingly a career aim for American players to win the national title.

The Open Championship is run by the Royal and Ancient Golf Club of St Andrews, regardless of where it is played. It is as admired for its organization as it is feared for its weather. It is by far the most international of the majors, with players competing from 40 or 50 countries. For that reason, as well as for its unrivalled tradition, it is often cited – even by Americans – as the premier tournament.

The last of the four majors, the US PGA Championship, is also the least, and is played on a different course each year. It is a predominantly American affair, and it suffers the disadvantage of usually being played in very hot August weather. It is organized by the Professional Golfers Association of America, and the field contains a large number of club professionals in addition to the top tour players and international stars. The lack of a comprehensive international field makes it the least prestigious of the four major championships.

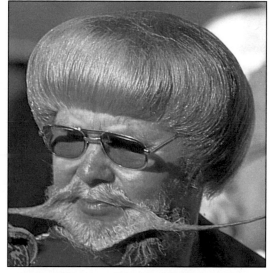
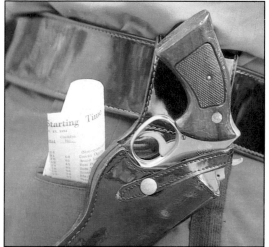

The Caddies

A top professional's caddie is far more than a simple porter. Of course he does carry the clubs, remove the flag stick and perform other highly visible tasks like holding an umbrella in the rain. But that is not where his job ends, or even begins.

Whether he arrives at the course with his player or, as often happens, a day earlier, the first thing a caddie does is to measure the course. If it is unfamiliar to him he will pace it out, step by step, noting everything that could have a bearing on play. Carelessness in this department could have disastrous consequences, and a good caddie knows that his livelihood depends solely on maintaining a reputation for accuracy and dependability.

The rewards can be considerable. The best caddies become essential fixtures in a player's routine, and they can expect to be treated with loyalty and generosity. They receive a salary, expenses and an agreed percentage of their player's winnings. Just as important, they quite naturally feel an important part of the professional golf scene. And when the winning putt goes in, they are far more than mere spectators at another's moment of triumph.

Right: A rare but welcome sight carrying clubs was Debbie Couples, caddying for her husband, Fred, during the 1982 US Open at Pebble Beach, California

It is unusual, but by no means unknown, for wives and relatives to act as caddies. Above left: Ossie Moore's wife, Mandy, used to caddie for him in his native Australia. Centre: The American Ken Green's sister, Shelley, caddied for him for most of the 1986 season.
Right: Fellow American David Ogrin celebrated the removal of club restrictions on caddies for the 1983 US Masters by appointing his sister, Alicia

Above: The distinguished American golf writer, Herbert Warren-Wind,
caddying for a kilted Ben Crenshaw during a
special visit to Hoylake. Crenshaw is a most dedicated
student of the history of the game, and was
demonstrating the art of playing with hickory clubs –
as well as the art of walking down the
fairway carrying a glass of whisky without spilling a drop

Below: Kilted caddies are a rare sight in the world of modern golf, but the sense of occasion at St Andrews for the 1984 Open Championship provided a photogenic excuse

Above: Vincente Ballesteros frequently caddies for brother Seve in major championships; in fact all three of the great Spaniard's brothers have performed this role. Note the two gold wristwatches – one obviously being sheltered from the power of the Ballesteros swing

Above: Jimmy Sullivan at the 1981 US Open needed a bag, and spotted Palmer. 'Who's carrying your bag then, Arnold?' Sully asked brashly. 'You are, if you want,' came the reply. Sully was rendered speechless

Above: Hubert Samuel Russell,
bills himself on his business
card 'Extraordinary Caddie'.
Who would argue, when he actually does
routinely carry the clubs on his head
while working at the Tryall Golf Club
in Jamaica? Right: Quiet contemplation
by a barefoot caddie in South Africa

Left: Brother James brings an Old Testament flavour to the US Open at Winged Foot in 1984. James Earl, to give him his real name, claims never to have cut his hair or beard, and to live his life by the three G's – God, golf and gardening.
Above: Caddies exchange greetings at Augusta National during the 1983 US Masters. Prior to that, tour caddies were not permitted to take part, which meant that caddies were all drawn from among the club's local black caddie staff

Below: 'Big Brian' peers down at 'Little Woosie', Britain's diminutive golfing phenomenon, Ian Woosnam

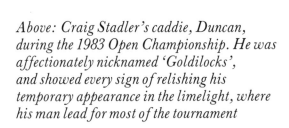

Above: Nicklaus with his British caddie, Jimmy Dickinson, at the end of the second round of the 1981 Open Championship at Royal St George's. After hearing that his son, Steve, had been injured in a car crash, Jack had shot a disastrous 81 in the opening round – and followed it with a blistering 66 to qualify

Above: Craig Stadler's caddie, Duncan, during the 1983 Open Championship. He was affectionately nicknamed 'Goldilocks', and showed every sign of relishing his temporary appearance in the limelight, where his man lead for most of the tournament

Above: Lee Trevino's British caddie, Willie Aitchison, has just willed that long putt into the hole during the 1983 Open Championship at Royal Birkdale

Above: Trevino's American caddie, Herman Mitchell, is in fact quite a useful golfer, but if he really wants to take this shot for his boss he could do with a golf club in his hands.
Left: Arnold Palmer's long-time Scottish caddie, Tip Anderson, raises a glass with his old friend and employer upon Palmer's arrival at St Andrews

The Spectators

The players create the excitement and drama, but the spectators provide the atmosphere. As in any sporting environment, that can be for better or worse, but golf is fortunate in having attracted crowds that are by and large knowledgeable. As a result, they are usually fair as well as enthusiastic.

There have recently been exceptions to this, and it is fervently hoped by all who love the game that this will not become a trend. When Seve Ballesteros hit his second shot into the lake in front of the 15th green in the final round of the 1986 Masters, the action was greeted by a resounding cheer from supporters of the charging Jack Nicklaus, despite the requests of Bobby Jones that this sort of behaviour should not happen at this event. And Europeans should not be over-hasty to point the finger at partisan American crowds. There was more than a little chauvanism in the air at The Belfry during the 1985 Ryder Cup. And as for the cheer that went up for Paul Azinger's wayward second shot on the final hole at Muirfield in 1987...

Having said that, it must be emphasized that spectators have a huge contribution to make to the sport. Not least, they provide the photographers with a welcome and colourful relief from those nail-biting 10-foot putts.

Right: Melbourne café society dressed to kill at the Victoria Open hosted by the Metropolitan Club. Centre: As for the chap pulling a face at Augusta, he belongs to a group of like-minded folk who do this sort of thing competitively. Far right: The Scottish gentleman would doubtless disapprove of both spectacles

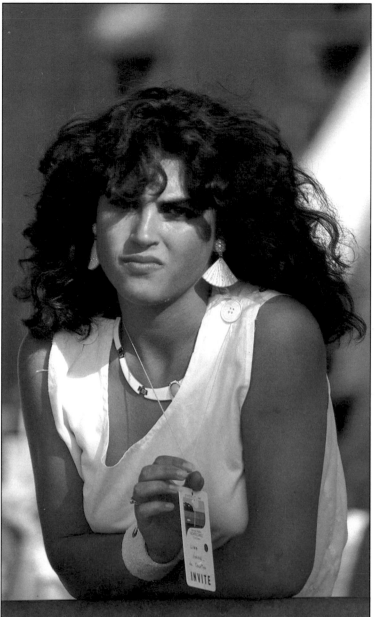

*Golf photographers never grow weary of the challenges provided
by the game itself, but that does not mean that their
camera's attention never wanders during lulls in the action.
Beautiful girls, whether blonde spectators, TV spotters for
American television networks, or scantily-clad scorers
attending the leader board occasionally come into focus, and
provide a welcome break from the ardours of covering the golf action*

131

Left: The electronic scoreboard typical of the PGA tour. Its computer graphics allow jolly little messages to be flashed to the crowd. Inset: Living proof that alligators really do 'love laying out on a day like this', at least at the Bay Hill Classic at Orlando, Florida. Right: Knowing that the legendary Rockin Rollen (Stewart) knows where to stand to be on television, other members crowd behind the 17th hole of the Bing Crosby Pro-Am at Pebble Beach. They send messages of greeting – and admonition – and compete for the television camera's attention

*Above: A quartet of pretty girls promotes the Bob Hope
Classic at Palm Springs, California.
At certain tournaments there are stern rules about
what the spectators may or may not do, but in this
case (above right) a distinctly waggish tee-shirt seems to
have escaped the course stewards' attention*

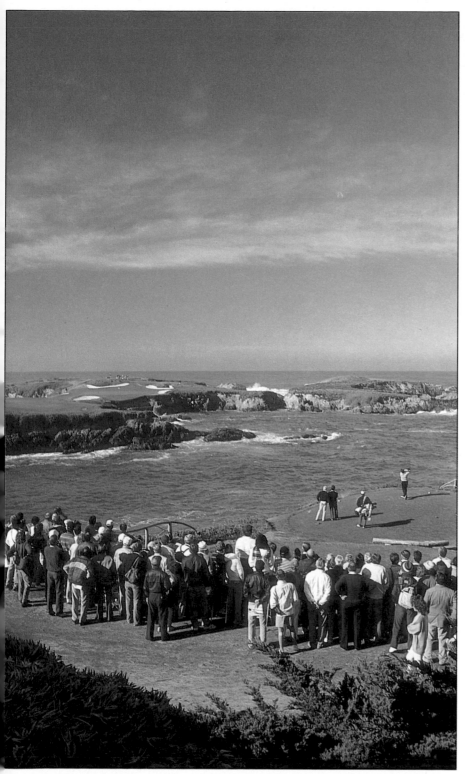

Left: One of the most photographed holes in golf, the 16th at Cypress Point, California, where the AT & T Pro-Am is held. Above: On a sunny day at Shinnecock Hills during the 1986 US Open, at least one spectator was prepared to take full advantage of the weather

Above: A Californian member of the golf photography fraternity sports a positively dangerous-looking waxed moustache. Right: The message must be one of the most wildly optimistic ever blazoned across a tee-shirt. It appeared at Augusta National on the Saturday of the US Masters, in the hope of drumming up spare tickets for the final day. Day trips to the moon would be more possible. Far right: Youngsters at Royal Birkdale improvise shelter during a typical English summer's day

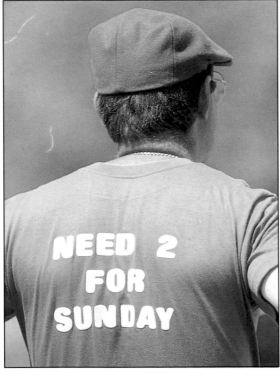

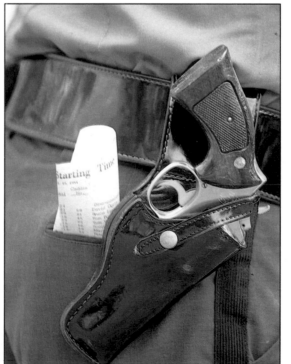

Strange sights on a golf course. Far left: This American 'beer hat' holds a goodly supply for the thirstiest spectator. Above: Even stranger and less practical head-gear at the Augusta National. Left: Also at Augusta, a paring sheet nestles beside a policeman's pistol

*Above: Signs and signals given to the golfing galleries of the world.
Quiet is paramount to a player's concentration, and volunteer marshalls at
the Bob Hope Classic in Palm Springs, California, are given the job of
calling for silence as the shots are played*

Left: At the Spanish Open at Marbella, the requests for quiet are given in their native tongue. Below: Walking standard bearers give information on the state of play. Right: At the Open Championship, formal attire, although not requested, is often worn to convey the same message

Scrapbook

In the sense that they perform for money, professional golfers are public people. Their wives, too, are in the public gaze whenever they accompany their husbands on tour. And on occasion they even join them on the course, for charity, and for a bit of light relief all around.

The private side of tour life is very much like any other travelling existence, where people who move around together and work together tend to socialize together. Photographers are part of the tour as well, and if now and again they take snapshots of the players off-duty, that is only to be expected . . .

In 1987, the tour wives played a charity tournament for the benefit of the Nancy Reagan Centre to Combat Alcohol and Drug Abuse at the Ponte Vedra Club. They raised $100,000. Far right: Barbara Nicklaus reacts to a stray shot while husband Jack shares the first green with the First Lady, special guest Nancy Reagan

The husbands caddied for their wives. Far left: Linda and Tom Watson look anxious, while Laura Norman and caddie Greg, (left), are naturally delighted with her 25-foot putt

*Vicki and Bernhard Langer walk
hand-in-hand down the fairway*

*A moment of high anxiety
for Claudia and Lee Trevino*

*Julie Crenshaw gets little
sympathy from her caddie, Ben*

Players and wives often have long hours to kill between rounds and although many of the wives find it difficult to fill in the time, there are a few events they would not like to miss. The trip to Hawaii during the winter is one such treat. Here Penny and Lanny Watkins enjoy a game of backgammon in the tropical setting of Kapalua

Left: Craig Stadler, 'The Walrus', and his son, Christopher, enjoy the warm Pacific at Kapalua, Hawaii. Above: Maurice Flitcroft is the infamous long-handicap amateur who has several times tried to compete in the Open Championship. In 1976 he entered posing as an American professional, but was found out after his first round of the qualifying when he scored over 120. He is pictured after that notorious round

Above: After a lifetime of the pressures of tournament golf, the immortal Sam Snead involves himself in a more leisurely pursuit before another Masters tournament. Right: English golfers enjoy the even more English game of cricket at Sandy Lyle's christening party for his son. From the left, Nick Faldo, Mark James, and Ian Woosnam at the crease

The Celebrities

Celebrities from all walks of life have taken to golf as a form of relaxation ever since the game was invented.

Bing Crosby and Bob Hope often rushed to Wentworth for a game of golf after filming had finished at Elstree, only to find that they had not had the time to remove all their make-up. It is these two golfing celebrities that can be credited with the birth of the Pro-Am tournament. Bob Hope's tournaments in Palm Springs, California, bring the top professionals and celebrities together with amateurs who are prepared to pay the $6000 entrance fee. They have raised millions of dollars for charity.

The late Bing Crosby's tournament was held on Monterey Peninsula in Northern California, but after his death, his wife, Kathryn, felt the tournament was becoming a corporate sideshow, and she made the decision to move the tournament with Bing's name to North Carolina. The tournament at Pebble Beach is now called the AT & T National Pro-Am – though to all those who knew and loved Bing, it will always be known as the Crosby.

The Four Stars National Celebrity tournament was started in 1985, and is the premier event of this type in Europe. It has brought with it the new type of golf fan, who comes to watch the celebrities as much if not more than the professionals themselves. Most regular tour events are preceded by a Pro-Am, but only in the Hope, the Crosby and the Four Stars do the amateurs have the opportunity to play all four rounds in competition with the professionals as partners.

Jack Lemmon is the most expressive of actors – and the most expressive of golfers. Left: The ecstasy as he holes his putt at the 18th in the 1987 AT & T Pro-Am at Pebble Beach. Right: The agony as he misses a putt during the same tournament. Jack has been known to turn down engagements in order to play in this, his favourite of all golfing events. Far right: Ex-president Gerald Ford is a golf fanatic and a danger to galleries whenever he plays on the Pro-Am circuit

Left: Kojak at a loss for once without his lollipop.
Telly Savalas is an annual competitor in the
Four Stars celebrity tournament. Right: The nattily
dressed Mickey Rooney in action in the Bob Hope Desert
Classic at Palm Springs, California.
Far right: Hollywood veteran Victor Mature surveys his tee
shot during the same event

*Above: Andy Williams, Pat Boone, Doug Sanders and George C Scott, all
competitors at Pebble Beach in the 1981 Crosby. Singers, actors and TV personalities
often lead lives suited to golf.
In the case of actors, they may have long resting periods between engagements.
Golf seems to give them the peace and tranquillity they need to recharge their batteries,
and many of them credit the game with maintaining their sanity
in the hectic show business world of travel and late nights*

Below: Singer Glen Campbell, one of the best celebrity swingers, is a regular on the US Pro-Am circuit. Travelling around the world, the stars have the opportunity to play the great courses, and some of them try to play in as many different places as possible, from the deserts of Africa to the famous Scottish links

Above: Howard Keel was one of the actors who managed to combine a business trip to London with his favourite pastime. He is pictured here at Moor Park having a game with professional Michael King, during the Four Stars event in 1985

151

*Left: Greg Norman helps the Mayor of Carmel,
Clint Eastwood, line up a putt when they
became partners in the AT & T Pro-Am in 1987.
Above: 77 Sunset Strip star Efrem Zimbalist
Junior shows he hasn't actually gone grey with age*

Above: James Garner plays off a five handicap at the Bel Air Country Club, and is a former winner of the Bob Hope British Classic.
Right: Bob Hope chats up Phyllis Diller

Above left: Conservative elder statesman
Lord Whitelaw is a keen golfer, and a former captain
of the Royal and Ancient Golf Club of St Andrews.
Above: Two of the hosts at the Four Stars event,
Jimmy Tarbuck and Terry Wogan, share
a joke at the presentation

Above left: Former British Heavyweight Champion, Henry Cooper, after holing a monster putt at Moor Park's 18th hole during the Four Stars where he is one of the host celebrities. Above right: Crooner Johnny Mathis proves that to sing is not the only way to swing

Above right: Peter Cook, who played in the celebrity section of the Million Dollar Golf Challenge in 1982, was asked why he was going to Sun City. 'For the sex, drugs and pornography, like everyone else,' came the reply

Left: Selwyn Nathan in caddie uniform while working for his friend, South African golfer Fulton Allem during the 1987 Open at Muirfield. Selwyn, a sports promoter from Johannesburg, had been negotiating with Seve Ballesteros to appear at the Million Dollar Golf Challenge at Sun City. Later that day Seve met Selwyn again in his caddie uniform on the practice ground. Seve looked disbelievingly at the sight before him. 'Why you do this?' he asked. Selwyn replied that he was doing it for fun. To which Seve retorted, 'No, for fun you go the beach.'

Right: With Greg Norman's passion for fast cars and Nigel Mansell's love of golf it was hardly surprising that these two great champions would become great friends. Here they are at the British Grand Prix at Silverstone the weekend before Greg's defence of his Open Championship at Muirfield. Greg and Nigel took off by helicopter after the final practice session to play a round at Woburn where they are pictured together along with a shot on the pit wall before the race

Caught out of uniform. Above: Ken Schofield and George O'Grady of the European PGA Tour relax over a quiet drink at the Four Stars Pro-Celebrity Tournament at Moor Park, Rickmansworth. Right and far right: Two giants of the golf industry: Deane Beman, the US PGA Tour Commissioner, and Mark McCormack, in golfing attire. The Commissioner spent his summer holiday playing golf in Europe and qualified for the Open Championship at Turnberry. Mark McCormack in action at the World Championship of Women's Golf Pro-Am showing loyalty to his clients by wearing a Rolex watch and an Arnold Palmer golf glove

Postscript

The last laugh. For all its seriousness, golf is, after all, just a game.
It gets harder and harder for players who rely on it for a living
to relax, so it is nice to see three of the greatest players
of all time having such fun while playing for big odds. Gary Player,
Jack Nicklaus and Arnold Palmer are pictured here during the filming of a small
television advertisement when Player could not seem to get his lines right

And so Brian and Lawrence, or as others call them Lawrence and Brian, walk off into the sunset. It is not the first sunset they have walked into, nor will it be their last. Throughout the golfing world Lawrence and Brian are celebrated for walking into things – doors, trees, the occasional truck – but momentary concussion has never impaired their work.

Ultimate professionals, they have never allowed unconsciousness to interfere with their work. Asleep or awake their photographic eye clicks continuously in anticipation of the unusual shot. Their methods are unorthodox: few photographers would disguise themselves as trees in pursuit of their art. Who can forget the famous weeping willow incident at the Claudette Colbert Desert Classic? On other occasions they have lain for hours under a thin layer of sand to further examine Nancy Lopez's bunker technique. And few people realize the amount of team work involved. It was Lawrence who took the picture of Jerry Pate emerging triumphant from the water, but it would not have been possible without Brian's shoulders on which Jerry was perched.

Their ability to transform themselves at a moment's notice into a 'Quiet Please' sign, a 'Positively No Admittance' or a divot, is the talk of the golfing world. Perhaps their most spectacular feat of camouflage is their staggeringly lifelike 'Ground Under Repair'. Many is the player who has unknowingly taken a free drop off one of these master photographers. They expect nothing in return except perhaps a free drop of this or a free drop of that at the clubhouse when it's all over. And after a few drops of this or a few drops of that, it's heads down for a preferred lie.

But even fast asleep on a snooker table their photographic minds are still clicking.

Peter Cook